WE HAVE TO
CHANGE

taking action to stabilize climate change,
curb population growth including immigration,
end poverty, and the liquidation of nature's capital

MARIA RONAY

iUniverse, Inc.
New York Bloomington

We Have to Change

iUniverse books may be ordered through booksellers or by contacting:

iUniverse
1663 Liberty Drive
Bloomington, IN 47403
www.iuniverse.com
1-800-Authors (1-800-288-4677)

Because of the dynamic nature of the Internet, any Web addresses or links contained in this book may have changed since publication and may no longer be valid. The views expressed in this work are solely those of the author and do not necessarily reflect the views of the publisher, and the publisher hereby disclaims any responsibility for them.

ISBN: 978-1-4502-7131-8 (sc)
ISBN: 978-1-4502-7133-2 (ebook)

Library of Congress Control Number: 2010916497

Printed in the United States of America

iUniverse rev. date: 11/11/2010

Preface

You probably already know that global warming is caused by man-made greenhouse gases that result mainly from the burning of fossil fuels (coal, natural gas, oil). But the world is also facing three other problems: liquidation of nature's capital, world poverty, and unsustainable population growth. These four enormous problems are interacting, each magnifying the severity of the other. And while the liquidation of nature's capital may be reversed to some extent, and world poverty is mainly a matter of money, climate change and population growth are irreversible; consequently they are the most severe of our problems and need to be addressed most urgently. This book suggests changes that world organizations, nations, and individuals should make in order for human civilization to survive.

The changes have to take place now. If we wait until a crisis comes, no time will be left for policy changes, research and development, nor will the wealth exist to pay for the enormous costs those programs would require.

Will we change?

It is up to you.

Contents

Chapter One
Where Are We Now?

Let us take an inventory of Earth.

Land

Firstly, in order to produce food, we need arable land. Currently, of the world's total land area (150 million square kilometers) about 10 percent is arable land. Meadows and pastures account for 24 percent, and forests and woodlands, 31 percent. The remaining 35 percent is either too dry, too cold, too hot, too rocky, too mountainous, or too poor in nutrients to be used for agriculture.

In addition to the use of pasture, more than half of US grain and about 40 percent of the world's grain is being fed to livestock rather than being consumed directly by humans. Producing one meat calorie requires ten to twelve grain calories, while animal protein is only 1.4 times as nutritious for humans as plant protein is.

Arable land is not a given; it is constantly created and destroyed. Its creation is a slow process; it may take hundreds of years for an inch-thick layer of topsoil to develop. The *destruction* of arable land, however, occurs much more quickly. The loss of land that is used for food, feed, and fiber is due mainly to the following:

- desertification;
- deforestation;
- erosion; or
- urbanization.

Desertification proceeds with an alarming rate, particularly in Africa and Asia, caused by droughts and overuse. If current trends of soil degradation continue in Africa, the continent might be able to feed just 25 percent of its population by 2025, according to the United Nations University Institute for Natural Resources in Africa. Nearly 80 percent of potentially cultivable arable land is now under cultivation in Asia.

Deforestation is harmful in more than one way.

Forests regulate water supply by absorbing rainfall and releasing it at a steady rate. As long as forests are intact, rivers transport water fairly uniformly throughout the year from their basins. If forests are cleared, the water supply changes from being fairly uniform to the alternating between floods and droughts. One of the consequences is that the floods wash away the soil from the steeper slopes, causing erosion. Deforestation also opens up areas to the devastation of wind. Because of deforestation on the slopes of the Himalayas, droughts are plaguing 500 million people in the Ganges valley and Bangladesh.

Increasingly important is the forest's role as a carbon sink; they absorb carbon dioxide, thus helping reduce greenhouse gases.

Deforestation is carried out to clear arable land, cut firewood, clear land for cattle, and grow biomass for ethanol. About an area of Greece (131,990 square kilometers) is lost to deforestation per year. The greatest loss is that of the tropical forests, some of the most valuable parts of Earth's ecosystem.

More than 90 percent of US cropland is losing soil to wind and water erosion at thirteen times the sustainable rate. Urbanization takes land for buildings, roads, and pavement. Urban land expansion and arable land loss are particularly great in China.

Agriculture requires fertilizers, herbicides, and pesticides, which in turn require energy to produce. In addition, their manufacture releases large amounts of greenhouse gases to the environment.

Both agriculture and animal husbandry require vast amounts of water.

Water

The greatest amount of water is required for agriculture and meat production. Nine hundred kilograms of water go into the production of one kilogram of wheat, whereas about twenty thousand kilograms of water go into the production of one kilogram of beef. This amounts to more than the use of water for thermoelectric generation, as well as industrial and domestic uses, with the proportions depending on the specific area.

A prime cause of the global water concern is the ever-increasing world population. As populations grow, industrial, agricultural, and individual water demands escalate. According to the World Bank, worldwide water demand is doubling every twenty-one years, more in some regions. Scores of countries are over-pumping aquifers as they struggle to satisfy their growing water needs, including each of the big three grain producers: China, India, and the United States.

More than half of the world's people live in countries where water tables are falling. Chinese wheat farmers in some areas are pumping from a depth of three hundred meters, or nearly a thousand feet. In the United States, the Department of Agriculture reports that in parts of Texas, Oklahoma, and Kansas, three leading grain-producing states, the water table dropped by more than thirty meters (one hundred feet) since large-scale irrigation began in the late 1940-s. Although this mining of underground water is taking a toll on US grain production, irrigated land accounts for only one-fifth of the US grain harvest, compared to close to three-fifths of the harvest in India and four-fifths in China.

In developing countries water shortage looms just as large as food shortage. More than 1 billion people lack access to potable water, and adequate sanitation is lacking for 2.4 billion people. About five million people die each year because of poor drinking water and lack of sanitation. Women and children in places all over the globe walk long hours to get a few liters of dirty water.

Air

Earth's atmosphere is a layer of gases surrounding the planet and containing roughly 78.08 percent nitrogen, 20.95 percent oxygen, 0.93 percent argon, 386 parts per million carbon dioxide, 1,745 parts per billion methane and 314 parts per billion nitrous oxide, together with a varying amounts of water vapor and some trace elements.

We are mainly concerned about the amount of greenhouse gases in the air. It is a lesser-known fact, that livestock is responsible for 18 percent of the world's greenhouse gas emissions as measured in carbon dioxide equivalents. By comparison, the world's entire transportation sector emits 13.5 percent of the carbon dioxide released into the atmosphere, while power plants emit 25 percent. Of course, these fractions depend on the degree of development for individual countries. For example in the United States, which produces about 23 percent of global greenhouse gases, agriculture accounts for 7 percent of total greenhouse gas emissions (in carbon dioxide equivalents), while transportation produces more than 25 percent, and power plants, about 40 percent.

There are however greenhouse gases other than carbon dioxide. Agriculture produces 65 percent of human-related nitrous oxide (which has 296 times the global warming potential of carbon dioxide) and 37 percent of all human-induced methane (which is twenty-three times more potent than carbon dioxide).

Because conditions change rapidly—alas, always for the worse—it is not possible to forecast the increase in the amount of greenhouse gases in the air from the trend representing the past twenty or thirty years. For example China overtook the United States in 2008 as the largest greenhouse gas producer in the world, despite the fact that five years ago, the nation was far behind. Also, in the past three to four years, the entire Siberian subarctic region began to melt. The sudden melting of the frozen peat bog, the size of France and Germany combined, could unleash billions of tons of methane into the atmosphere.

Global Warming

Unfortunately climate change is already here. Subtropical regions expanded northward, yielding increased aridity in the southern United States, the Mediterranean region, Australia, and parts of Africa. Impacts of this climate shift reveal that the carbon dioxide level (386 parts per million) is already causing much harm.

Alpine glaciers retreat, bringing with them dry rivers for the summers. As temperatures in the Arctic warmed at three times the global average, last summer the Arctic lost more sea ice than ever before, amounting to the combined land areas of Texas and California. Increasing ice mass losses in Greenland and West Antarctica also increase concerns about ice stability, leading to a rising sea level and the potential acceleration of global warming.

Oil

Oil reserves are the estimated quantities of crude oil recoverable under existing economic and operating conditions. Crude oil reserves are estimated to be about 990 billion barrels, or, if Canadian oil sands under active development are included, then the world's proven oil reserves in 2007 according to *Oil & Gas Journal* are 1,317 billion barrels of oil. Dividing this with a yearly oil production of twenty-five to thirty billion barrels, we can predict the reserves will last forty-four to fifty-three years, assuming no increase in yearly production.

The major use of oil is in transportation; gasoline, jet fuel, and diesel provide more than 95 percent of all fuel used by cars, trucks, aircraft, trains, ships, agricultural, and industrial machinery. Oil is also used as the starting material for many chemicals, pharmaceuticals, synthetic materials, and so on, and it is used (to a decreasing extent) for the production of electricity and heating.

There are about 850 million cars in the world today, including commercial vehicles. There are 251 million cars, SUVs, and light trucks registered in the United States with a fuel efficiency of seventeen to twenty-two miles per gallon. It is in the transportation sector, particularly in passenger cars, that substitution of oil products is the most problematic. Two popular alternatives, hydrogen and corn ethanol, are less than good alternative fuels. Hydrogen has to be produced from the electrolysis of water (today it is derived from fossil fuel, which defeats the purpose); this requires very much energy, though renewable energy sources like solar, wind, or atomic energy can be used for this purpose. Hydrogen is very light; therefore it has to be compressed or liquefied to obtain sufficient mass. It forms explosive and flammable mixtures with air in a broad range of concentrations. It diffuses through most materials due to the small size of the hydrogen molecule and embrittles many metals, including steel, further increasing the danger of storing it under high pressure in a passenger car. Hydrogen would require a totally new and very expensive infrastructure for distribution.

Roughly one gallon gasoline equivalent of fossil fuel is used to produce 1.5 gallons of ethanol from corn. Since its energy is only two-thirds that of gasoline, fundamentally 1.5 gallons of ethanol is needed to replace 1 gallon of gasoline, which is used to produce it, thus the energy gain is zero. The environmental loss, however, is huge. Corn produces more soil erosion than any other US crop; and it needs more irrigation, fertilizer, herbicide, and pesticide than any other crop, thus causing more water pollution. In 2008 nearly one-third of the US grain harvest was going to ethanol. Since the United States is the leading exporter of grain, what happens to the US grain crop affects the entire world. Exports will drop. The UN currently lists thirty-four countries as needing emergency food assistance. People are dying of hunger. Using corn ethanol for car fuel is bad environmental engineering at best and immoral human behavior at worst.

Natural Gas

Proven reserves of natural gas are at 180 trillion cubic meters, which would supply the world at the current rate of consumption for about seventy years. The major part of natural gas is methane (chemical formula: CH_4). Because of its high hydrogen content, it adds the smallest amount of carbon dioxide to the atmosphere as compared to the other two primary fossil fuels, petroleum oil and coal. It is clean-burning and flexible and has a high energy content. The major sources are in the Middle East and Russia. Transport may take place through pipelines, but when being moved over large distances or across seas, natural gas has to be liquefied, transported in huge tankers, and re-gasified. Each step is costly and consumes large amounts of energy. In addition there are safety concerns associated with all of these steps.

There are nonconventional sources of natural gas, as well, representing larger resources like coal bed methane, tight sands, and shales; however, the extraction of natural gas from these sources is more expensive and rises some environmental concerns. Methane hydrates exist in vast quantities at great depths, for example, in the oceanic sediments of continental slopes and the continental shelves of seas; but exploration of these sources is still in the research stage.

Natural gas is increasingly replacing coal in electricity generation and replacing oil in residential domestic applications. It is used for the production of hydrogen, and from hydrogen, through ammonia, for the production of fertilizers. While petrochemicals (which constitute the building blocks for many chemicals, pharmaceuticals, and synthetic materials) can be easily and economically produced from petroleum, they can also be manufactured from methane, although this is less efficient and requires a greater expenditure of energy.

Coal

Recoverable coal reserves are estimated at about 900 gigatons (one gigaton equals one billion tons). World coal consumption is about 6.2

gigatons annually; at the current consumption rate, this would last roughly 150 years. The largest coal reserves are in the United States (27.1 percent), followed by Russia (17.3 percent), China (12.6 percent), and India (10.2 percent). Many other countries around the world have smaller coal reserves; the largest coal producer and user, however, is China. Worldwide about 75 percent of coal consumption goes toward the production of electricity; 51 percent of US electricity comes from coal-fired power plants.

Coal-fired power stations are the least carbon efficient in terms of the carbon dioxide produced per unit of electricity generated. In addition to emitting the most carbon dioxide, they also emit significant levels of pollutants, such as sulfur dioxide and nitrogen oxides (which cause acid rain) as well as arsenic and the heavy metals mercury, lead, and uranium, all of which pose health hazards. Modern coal-fired power plants have improved efficiency and emit reduced amounts of pollutants, but due to their long life (seventy-five years), even developed countries have plenty of old ones. Unfortunately China now opens a new coal-powered power station every week; in addition, it does not buy modern equipment from the West, and instead secures polluting, low-efficiency equipment from other sources.

The high temperature needed for cement manufacturing makes it an energy-intensive process. Large amounts of coal are used in cement manufacturing, and here again, China is the leading producer with 1.3 gigatons of cement manufactured annually (that is, one ton of cement for every Chinese person) with the concomitant carbon dioxide and pollutant release.

Population

In 1950 Earth's population was still at 2.5 billion. Then came an enormous jump in population. The populations of the most populous countries are shown along with the world population for 1950 and 2009, and as predicted for 2050. The numbers (obtained from GeoHive) are given in millions and are rounded to the million.

1950		2009		2050	
China	562	China	1,335	India	1,808
India	370	India	1,158	China	1,424
USA	152	USA	305	USA	420
Russia	102	Indonesia	239	Indonesia	313
Japan	84	Brazil	198	Pakistan	295
World	2,556	World	6,750	Bangladesh	280
				Ethiopia	278
				Nigeria	264
				Brazil	261
				DR Congo	189
				World	9,539

The term *total fertility rate* refers to the average number of children born to women during their childbearing years. Two children per woman would replace the parents, but because slightly more boys than girls are born, and because some children die, the replacement fertility rate for countries with good healthcare is an average of 2.1 children per woman. When women have more children than the replacement fertility rate, the population grows. Even with a growth rate (as percentage of population) of 2 percent per year, a country's population doubles in thirty-five years. But even if a replacement fertility rate is reached, it takes three generations, or, roughly one life expectancy (sixty-six years worldwide) to reach zero population growth due to so-called population momentum. In China a mandatory one-child policy was introduced in 1980, and while the country's fertility rate is currently 1.6, the population is still increasing at a rate of 0.6 percent per year.

Few people realize that according to the 2005–2010 list by the UN, the United States has the largest population growth rate among large developed countries at 0.97 percent. This is due to immigration and the high fertility rate of immigrant women. If current trends continue, the US population will rise from 308 million in 2009 to 420 million in 2050. Over 80 percent of this increase will be attributable to new immigrants arriving after 2005 and to their descendants. For example the fertility rate of Mexican women in the United States is 3.5 children, compared to 2.3 children per woman in Mexico. (The total fertility rate for the world is 2.6 children per woman.)

Apart from the United States, most of the population growth will take place in the developing countries with the highest population growth rates in the Middle East and Africa. Some of the most troubled countries in these regions are experiencing explosive population growth. Wars are most often fought over resources like food and water, and increasing populations have increasing needs. Since 1960, when the world population passed the 3 billion mark, several countries need regular international aid in food. Currently about one billion of the world's people are malnourished, and six million children die annually as a consequence of hunger.

The Ecological Footprint, conceived in 1990 by Mathis Wackernagel and William Rees, has emerged as an important measure of humanity's demand on nature. It gauges the amount of resources, land, and water that a human population requires to produce the goods and services, such as food, fiber, seafood, timber, paper, settlements, and energy, that it consumes and to absorb its waste products (carbon dioxide, garbage, etc.) in a sustainable way so that the planet can support a population of similar size in the future.

Due to population growth and increasing per capita consumption, since the 1980s, humanity has been in an ecological overshoot with annual demand on resources exceeding what the planet can regenerate in a year. It now takes Earth one year and four months to regenerate what we use in one year. We maintain this overshoot by liquidating Earth's resources, its natural capital. Many forms of natural capital are irreplaceable on a time scale that would be of interest to humanity. Coral reefs, which are sources of seafood, agricultural soils, biodiversity (by providing agricultural ecosystem services such as maintenance of soil fertility, pollination, pest control), ancient forests, and groundwater may take hundreds of years to replace, while the replacement of fossil fuels takes *millions* of years.

If a population, in this case the global human population, is being supported, not by the income from natural capital, but by increasing depletion of the capital itself, there is overpopulation.

Chapter Two
The Danger Ahead

According to James Hansen, director of NASA's Goddard Institute for Space Studies, and his collaborators paleoclimate evidence and ongoing climate change suggest that the carbon dioxide content of the atmosphere will need to be reduced from its current concentration of 386 parts per million to at most 350 parts per million. If we do not ensure that the present overshoot of this target is brief in duration, we may seed irreversible, catastrophic effects.

As evidenced by droughts, floods, and melting Arctic and Antarctic ice, climate change is already here; the current carbon dioxide level of 386 parts per million is already doing much harm. Man-made climate change is delayed by ocean and ice-sheet response times, and as shown by the above scientists, warming that is in the pipeline, so to speak, mostly attributable to these slow feedbacks, is now about two centigrade above the pre-industrial global temperature, at the limit of what we can endure. Judging from paleoclimate history, the equilibrium sea level rise for 386 parts per million, also in the pipeline, is at least several meters.

Scientists advising the International Panel on Climate Change (IPCC) suggested a similar goal and estimated that a 60 to 80 percent reduction in carbon dioxide emissions from the 1990 level would result in a stabilization of the atmospheric concentration of that gas at 353 parts per million, a level which apparently does not cause climate change. Why do we have to reduce to below the 1990 emissions? Because we are at 386 parts per million, and in order to get down to 353 parts per million, we must now emit less than in 1990.

The 1990 carbon dioxide emission rate for the world was 22.3 gigatons per year (a gigaton equals a billion tons); reducing this by 60 percent means we can emit 40 percent of this amount per year, that is, 8.9 gigatons. It is more convenient to calculate in carbon equivalents. Since 3.666 gigatons of carbon dioxide is equivalent to one gigaton of carbon, our planet has to reduce its yearly carbon emission to 2.4 gigatons per year (8.9/3.666), about the same amount the planet was emitting in 1960, when the world's population was only three billion.

Emitting 2.4 gigatons of carbon per year is roughly equivalent to emitting one part per million of carbon dioxide per year. If current carbon sinks (oceans, forests, and so on) are still active at former levels, then more carbon dioxide will be absorbed than the emitted one part per million per yr, and in many years, the current level in the atmosphere will be reduced to the desired 353 parts per million.

This, however, is a formidable task. US emissions increased in parallel with population. In 2007, per capita carbon emissions level in the United States was 5.44 tons. If the US population keeps growing at the current rate, and per capita emissions remain the same, by 2050 the annual emissions of the United States alone will exceed the global limit of 2.4 gigatons per year. It is clear that the United States must reduce both its population growth and per capita emission.

Even if the per capita emission in China is only 1.46 tons per year, this figure multiplied by China's immense population of 1.335 billion people amounts to a 1.95-gigaton carbon emission over the course of a year. This is currently increasing by 11 percent annually. If uncurbed, *within two years* China will emit 2.4 gigatons per year—the amount that is allotted for the entire planet.

There are nations like China, which had belated industrial revolutions but were overpopulated in previous years. There are nations with large per capita emissions but stable and manageable populations (Europe, Japan). And then there is the United States, which has the largest per capita emissions and the largest population growth among developed nations.

How should the permissible amount of carbon emissions be allocated? Ultimately the only fair method would be to divide the 2.4-gigaton carbon allowance by the world's population (2.4/6.75 billion = 0.355 ton of carbon per capita). This is what has to be achieved—and it is a frighteningly small number.

France—which gets 80 percent of its electricity from nuclear power, closed its last coal mine in 2004, and manufactures the highest mileage cars—emits 1.64 tons per capita. While this is only 30 percent of US emissions, it is almost five times as much as what can be allocated for every human being in the near future. Clearly our carbon emission goal could have been more easily accomplished if the world's population remained at the 1960 level of three billion, in which case the personal allowance would be 2.0 tons of carbon per year. On the other hand if the population grows in excess of 9.5 billion by midcentury, as predicted, humans will not be able to live with a carbon-emission quota of only a quarter ton. Bear in mind that the poor of these anticipated 9.5 billion people (more than half of that total) will be better fed, will eat more meat, and will be able to purchase more goods and energy.

So far we have only talked about the estimated annual amount of carbon emissions coming from the burning of fossil fuels, oil and derivatives, natural gas, and coal, that is compatible with the stabilization of atmospheric carbon dioxide. This puts most of the blame on developed nations. But developing nations, which keep animals (livestock is responsible for 18 percent of the world's greenhouse emissions), grow rice (rice paddy fields are a major source of methane emissions, a greenhouse gas twenty-three times more potent than carbon dioxide), and cook with inefficient wood-burning stoves (estimated to put 0.6 ton of carbon per capita per year into the air), and which in total account for an immense portion of the world population, are also putting significant amounts of greenhouse gases into the atmosphere.

Apart from, but not independent of, climate change, population growth is increasingly eliminating Earth's capital. More tropical forests are cut down, more soils are cultivated (or built on), and more groundwater is used. More oil wells and mineral mines are depleted. But the damage to nature is not proportional to the increase in population. The easiest sources were depleted first. The land on which agriculture is extended is poorer; the water comes from greater depth; sources of fossil fuels and minerals are more difficult to access. This causes disproportionately more environmental damage. Climate change, by causing droughts and floods, is further increasing the environmental damage.

The number of people living in poverty is currently about three billion. Generally, people living in poverty have the largest population growth; inasmuch as this is a result of conscious decisions, it is partially due to social reasons (in traditional agrarian societies, which most poor nations are, children provide free labor and support parents in old age) and to compensate for high infant mortality but also, mainly, because of a lack of family planning information and services.

The exploding poor population takes a tremendous toll on nature. In order to assure their survival, people destroy forests to make place for agricultural or grazing land and to obtain firewood for cooking. The lands that are thus cultivated are very vulnerable ecologically. The consequence of disappearing forests is flooding, as seen in India, Bangladesh, and the countries of Southeast Asia, while overgrazing, soil erosion, and desertification bring famine. This occurred in the Sahel region of Africa in the 1970s, resulting in three hundred thousand deaths. But the phenomenon is not limited to Africa; it is spreading around the world.

Perhaps the greatest danger posed by the increasing population is that hundreds of millions of malnourished people with weakened immune systems live in ever closer proximity with more and more animals, both domesticated ones and those encountered in land clearing. These conditions greatly increase the probability of a disease mutating and passing from animals to humans. Due to crowded living conditions and a lack of health care, such new diseases would spread within the poor population and then, due to global traffic, to the developed world as well (think HIV/AIDS), creating epidemics of unheard severity. What will people do when millions of starving and ill people storm the borders of the better-off countries?

If humanity wants to prevent the greatest tragedies it has ever encountered—unimaginable natural disasters, hundreds of millions of starving environmental refugees, tragedies from which many people will die and after which no one will be able to lead a civilized life—then it has to face the facts and act now. These dangers are facing mankind:

1. Climate change
2. Liquidation of nature's capital
3. World poverty

These three interact with each other in a way that magnifies the problem. The fourth—population growth—is immensely accelerating the liquidation of nature's capital and of world poverty.

Huge and growing populations will immensely accelerate climate change. These are the problems that need to be solved for mankind to survive. Climate change can be impacted by reducing the carbon emissions of developed nations. Such a change can take place in a short time. Emergencies can reduce consumption very quickly. But population growth is different. Once children are born, they increase the population for three generations.

Chapter Three
The Age of Healing

Us

After pursuing the hunter-gatherer way of life about ten millennia ago, people started to cultivate the land for grains and domesticate animals, and the agricultural age began. The surplus food made the division of labor and specialization possible; thus cultures and states slowly developed, and professional soldiers fought wars against other states. Wars were fought mainly for resources such as land, water, and goods, which were now other people's properties. The population grew, and land was abused, forests were cut down, land was over irrigated causing salinization. But since Earth's population was small, the abuses caused only local problems.

The industrial age started in the late eighteenth century, when goods were manufactured in factories with the aid of machines, making them cheaper and available to more people. Industry, transportation, and energy production were propelled by the burning of fossil fuels, mainly coal. It was still possible to provide for the population of Earth in a sustainable way since the population was not overly large and only a fraction of the population was consuming more than before.

Both the agricultural age and the industrial age remain with us today (supplemented by the Information Age) with the difference being that the population is immense. Each person wants to consume more and more, and the damage done to Earth and to the atmosphere is felt all around the world.

It is not possible to provide even for Earth's current population without destroying the climate and the ecosystem of the planet and changing it to a place that is unsuitable for civilized human life.

The solution to this problem is not to be found in science and technology alone. The current deterioration is not the result of a natural catastrophe or devastation by alien armies; it is the consequence of our own behavior, values, lifestyles, actions, and, most important, our thoughtlessness. Therefore, the downward spiral can only be halted if we ourselves change.

We have to enter the age of healing: healing the ecosystem, the climate of Earth, and ourselves.

The sixth commandment says, "Thou shall not kill." In a broader sense the commandment forbids us to endanger the lives of others. We know that damaging the climate and the ecosystem causes natural disasters, such as famines, from which many people have died. Unnecessary consumption and unaffordable fertility harms other people and contributes to the misery and death of many.

Each of us living today has to undergo a paradigm change, see things in a different way than before, and select values and actions with the guiding question being whether or not it does harm to the planet and to the people who depend on it. The change must be different for people who live in developed countries enjoying affluence than for those living in poverty and mostly without rights in underdeveloped countries.

For those who are affluent, the aim of life is not to fulfill our ever increasing material "needs," ever increasing need for entertainment, comfort, "freedom" of action in the service of self-interest, or ruthless competition to win material prizes but to find a true human existence, rich in intellectual and ethical achievement; to see those aspects of life that were so far hidden from us, to learn about nature and about people living far away; to be understanding, compassionate, and helpful; to make the immense intellectual, moral, and political effort necessary to avoid the catastrophe facing mankind; to feel responsible for the entire planet, to be cosmopolitan instead of individualistic, and to realize that true freedom means not to conquer what can be conquered, but to choose what is good.

As Jimmy Carter said, a person has to be judged not by what he owns but by what he does. We have to disapprove of rather than admire excess, look with disdain at McMansions, and hope that instead of those and slums, there will be safe and healthy accommodations for all. We should look with contempt at SUVs (if not at their owners) and work toward a dramatic decrease in the idolization and use of the personal automobile.

We must travel less by air—no hopping to Hawaii for the weekend. One vacation per year involving air travel should do. An airplane emits on the order of fifty kilograms of carbon per passenger per thousand miles. That is a large fraction of one's yearly allowance (355 kilograms of carbon). Buy voluntary carbon offsets from the airline. Watch travel programs on television instead of going to faraway places. You cannot see landscapes in person on your own from the vantage points from which they filmed, nor can you see art in major museums without standing in line and fighting crowds.

We must eat less meat, particularly beef. One day a week without meat is a good start. Have baked beans instead (okay, you can add a little bacon). And feel sorry for the beautiful young woman who marries a rich old man instead of a young reformer with a purpose and shining eyes.

For women living in poverty, learning and having equal rights to men (who, themselves, should have more rights) is essential. Most important, women should be able to decide when to have children and how many of them. A great number of childbirths endanger the health of poor women. Also, these women become vessels, caregiving is their sole activity, having no time or energy left to fulfill their own selves, to have professions, jobs, to become whole people.

A woman can take better care of fewer children; she can feed them better and get them better health care and education. She, as well as all other women, should be content having two healthy children.

If she has love and energy left, she should give it to her neighbor's children.

She must not think that she has to have many children because she is sure many of them will die in childhood. This is exactly the tragedy that the world has to fight to avoid. She should not think that many children will better support her in old age; it is usually just one child who shoulders the burden; furthermore nation states will have to provide for some measure of old age security.

She should be given counsel and access to contraception, but beyond that, it should be her own decision. She should not be coerced by governments to have fewer children or coerced—by husbands, lovers, or most important, enemy soldiers—to have unprotected sexual encounters that will result in unwanted pregnancies.

All this requires governments' commitment to family planning and to having numerous clinics providing reproductive health services (for births and infant care as well as contraception), all with the massive aid of developed countries, because this will be the first step toward reducing world poverty.

Men must study and become informed and try to carve out modern lives for themselves. They must stop fighting medieval wars with medieval cruelty, and fight instead for rights—and then share them with women.

All this requires great help from developed countries, less in the form of financial aid, which is so often squandered by corruption, but rather in the form of investments to improve agricultural yield, heath care, education, and infrastructure.

The World

The world is facing four large problems: climate change, liquidation of nature's capital, world poverty, and population growth. These problems can only have global solutions, requiring a global institution that collects data, raises public awareness, gathers experience from small-scale trials, and initiates a global framework for action. Luckily we have such an organization: the United Nations.

In addition to a diplomatic role, best known through the actions of the UN Security Council, and being the provider of peacekeeping and emergency relief operations when national governments are unable or unwilling to provide these services, the UN is the keeper of shared commitments on global objectives, such as the UN Framework Convention on Climate Change, the UN Environmental Program, the UN Convention on Biodiversity, the UN Convention to Combat Desertification, the UN Development Program, the UN Millennium Project, the UN Population Fund, the UN Children's Fund, and so on. For the sake of solving the enormous global problems facing humanity, we should all learn as much as possible about the work of the UN, and support it in every way.

For the participating countries (192 in all) the position of the ambassador to the UN should be a very important one, perhaps the third most important government position after president and vice president (or prime minister where applicable), commensurate with the importance of the problems the UN deals with.

— *Climate change*

In order to avoid a global warming in excess of two degrees centigrade we have to reduce the global carbon emissions to between 20 and 40 percent of 1990 global emissions by 2050. In a previous example we used a reduction to 40 percent. Let us make it clear that the developed countries have to reduce their emissions to their allocated fraction of the reduced 1990 *global* emissions and not merely to their own

1990 emissions rates reduced by the same percentage. This is a huge difference.

One might think that 2050 is far away, but it is not so. To achieve this goal by 2050 is a Herculean task. It is important to note, that the above stated goal can only be achieved by 2050 if global carbon emissions peak as soon as possible, meaning that they do not increase from now on.

Before suggesting global actions, we have to give some thought to how we got into this dangerous situation. Developed countries get a lot of blame, and indeed they did and do emit large amounts of carbon. But its harmful effects on the climate were not well known and accepted before the 1990s, at which time remedial actions were initiated.

A larger problem is the population explosion in the developing nations. If the world's population had remained at its 1950 level (2.5 billion), there would be no climate change, ecological disasters, large-scale deforestation, desertification, or shortages of water or food. There would be significantly less poverty and fewer wars. But, unlike the effect of greenhouse gases on climate, the ill effects of population growth were discussed beginning in the end of the eighteenth century, and indeed common sense would make the connection between population size and the capacity of Earth to provide for it. Yet, for example, China's population grew by 773 million people between 1950 and 2009 (see the table); India's grew by 778 million people.

While China made stringent and successful efforts in the 1980s to stabilize its population, due to the population momentum its population is still growing (although not as much as if the country had not made those changes). By 1955, India had taken some tentative steps to slow population growth; in 1976, authorities forcibly sterilized some people in high-fertility rural areas, making news of the family planning movement's excesses, and India's national family planning program has not recovered since.

By 2050, the combined population of China and India is predicted to be 3.2 billion; add to this the expected 1.5-2 billion people of Sub-

Saharan Africa, 700 million of the Middle East and North Africa, and you have to realize that the developing nations will have a much larger impact on climate change, than the developed ones. *The first and most urgent task that must be taken toward the mitigation of climate change is stabilizing the world's population; this will have both the largest and the longest-lasting impact on climate change.*

To be fair we will have to divide the 2050 yearly carbon emission allowance for Earth by the number of people living on the planet then. As shown previously, with the current population this allows for 0.355 ton of carbon per capita (or 355 kilograms carbon per capita) per year (2.4/6.75).

This is a very small number; current US emissions are 5.44 tons per capita per year. Other developed countries, with the exception of France, are not very far behind. This decrease, of more than an order of magnitude, can only be achieved with a carbon tax in the developed nations.

The developing nations must not go down the same road that the developed nations did during nineteenth- and twentieth-century industrialization; if they do, they will destroy Earth's climate in no time because of their immense populations. This road can only be avoided with the introduction of a carbon tax in the developing nations as well.

Of all the different kinds of electricity-producing plants, coal-fired power plants are the largest carbon emitters; thus it is critical that carbon is captured on the spot and sequestered in appropriate locations, for example, in geological formations or under the ocean floor. More often than not, this will also require transportation. No large-scale experiments on carbon capture and sequestration (CCS) have been done yet, and it is expensive. Furthermore, because an automobile fleet that uses renewable energy is still decades away and because air and water transportation will still make use of fossil fuels, we must also remove carbon dioxide from the ambient air. Since the carbon dioxide concentration is the same everywhere on Earth, this can be done at locations near safe storage sites.

Currently the capture of carbon dioxide from the ambient air is predicted to cost on the order of $200 per ton of carbon. This is very expensive, and private industry will not invest in it; but a carbon tax can pay for it.

No matter how attractive wind and solar energy are—and private industry can be expected to take care of those investments—it will not provide all the energy the planet's population needs. A great fraction of the energy needed by both developing and developed nations must be provided by nuclear energy—this is unavoidable. Currently there are 436 nuclear fission reactors, out of which only eleven are in China and seventeen in India, providing for a paltry 16 percent of the world's current energy needs. The number of nuclear fission reactors must be greatly increased. The cost per reactor is over $10 billion, and it is questionable that private industry will invest in it.

The objective of the carbon tax is to remove carbon from the atmosphere or prevent it from getting into the atmosphere. The magnitude of the carbon tax should reflect what it costs to remove carbon from the atmosphere or to prevent it from getting into the atmosphere. *The collected carbon tax must be spent to remove carbon from the atmosphere, or to prevent it from getting into the atmosphere.*

Due to the magnitude of the necessary carbon reduction, we cannot succeed in this endeavor any other way, nor can we influence individual and business behavior without it.

Nuclear fusion energy lies further in the future. Nuclear fusion does what the sun does: converts hydrogen to helium at extremely high temperatures. Here on Earth we apply burning plasmas, very hot fully ionized gases. The high temperature is maintained primarily through self-heating from fusion reactions within the plasma.

Most fusion reactions combine isotopes of hydrogen to form isotopes of helium. Because the mass of the reaction products is less than the mass of the reacting ones, and the difference is transformed to energy, this energy is an order of magnitude greater than that created by nuclear fission from the same amount of (but different kind of) starting material.

The reaction is inherently safe, neither the starting material: the hydrogen isotopes deuterium and tritium, (made by breeding from lithium) nor the end product helium is toxic or radioactive. Nuclear fusion energy is clearly the energy source of the future.

There is an international collaboration to put reactor-scale physics and technology together. The goal of ITER (International Thermonuclear Experimental Reactor) is to demonstrate that a fusion power plant is feasible. The starting materials, deuterium (found in seawater) and lithium, are both abundant on Earth. The plasma is confined in a tokamak (an acronym made of Russian words), which is a torroidal chamber with a magnetic field.

ITER's 15-billion-euro budget for constructing the experiment is shared by the EU and six non-host countries. The United States zeroed the funding of $150 million for 2008, and restored it to $124 million for 2009.

A full-scale power plant is planned to come on line in 2050, assuming that ITER demonstrates that the tokamak type of magnetic confinement is the most promising for power generation. While it will not be easy to bring this date forward, an increased intellectual and financial investment may do so.

At the other end of the spectrum of what technology can do is the reduction of black carbon, a particulate air pollutant formed by the incomplete combustion of fossil fuels, biofuels, and biomass.

In Africa and Asia black carbon is produced by wood-dung-burning stoves used by hundreds of millions of poor people. The burning of forests and savannas is another major contributor. The use of diesel fuel in America and Europe also creates black carbon. Black carbon causes global warming in two ways: When in the atmosphere, the particles absorb sunlight and emit it as heat. Also, after being carried to the Arctic by winds, the carbon particles fall on the snow and ice, darken it, and reduce the ability of originally white surfaces to reflect sunlight, causing the ice and snow to melt.

One of the greatest dangers of global warming is the melting of Arctic ice. The average temperature in the Arctic has risen by 2 degrees centigrade over the past forty years – much higher than the global average. Black carbon is responsible for 50 percent of the total temperature increases in the Arctic, amounting to a full degree centigrade.

Because black carbon stays in the atmosphere only for days and weeks, reducing its production would have immediate payoff and an instant effect on reducing the melting of Arctic ice. So far this is the single piece of good news that we have in the realm of climate change.

Since 25 to 35 percent of black soot comes from China and India, international agreements should require these nations to reduce it in their respective countries.

Developed countries, in addition to further regulating diesel exhausts, need to help Africa. Solar-powered cooking stoves cost twenty dollars apiece; the United States Agency for International Development (USAID) could distribute hundred million of them under existing programs, or better still, set up manufacturing of the stoves in Africa.

– *Preserving nature's capital*

Our survival depends on ecosystems, natural systems that supply us with food, fresh water, clean air, and a stable climate and that protect us from disease and disaster. Is there anything else more important? Yet the Millennium Ecosystem Assessment, a study conducted for four years by 1,360 experts, found that Earth will not be able to support current and future generations.

Ecosystem services provide food, fresh water, timber, and fiber for clothing; they protect us from extreme weather, floods, fire, and disease; and they regulate Earth's climate, filter wastes and pollutants, regenerate clean air, water, and soil, and inspire spiritual, artistic, and recreational activities.

Some 60 percent of the ecosystems examined, including fisheries and fresh water, are being degraded and used in unsustainable ways. These changes are magnified by climate change, population growth, and increasing per capita consumption. They are felt the most by poor populations and prevent the reaching of UN development goals. Plans to eradicate famine and disease worldwide cannot be accomplished as expected while such environmental damage occurs.

The Millennium Assessment says that we cannot treat nature as free and limitless anymore but must put a value on natural systems and their irreplaceable contributions to human well-being. While the Millennium Assessment found, that it is possible to make changes that would mitigate many of these problems, not enough effort is made to include the necessary policies.

Biodiversity, the variety among living creatures, is an important feature of healthy ecosystems because it increases their flexibility and resilience. In view of the changing climate, the capacity of ecosystems to adjust to change is most valuable. Over the past centuries humans increased the extinction rate of species as much as a thousandfold due to deforestation, overgrazing, desertification, monocultural agriculture, loss of mangroves and coral reefs, pollution, and so on.

The world's tropical forests have the greatest biological diversity and may contain plants that could yield medicines to cure cancer, AIDS, and other illnesses. Currently a quarter of our medicines are derived from plant sources, yet we let the tropical forests be cut down, extinguishing plants that we do not know the benefits of. The United Nations Convention on Biological Diversity (CBD) called for action in 1992 to conserve biodiversity. The resulting treaty's goals, adopted in 2002, were "to achieve by 2010 a significant reduction of the current rate of biodiversity loss at the global, regional and national level as a contribution to poverty alleviation and to the benefit of all life on Earth." Not much happened, and this goal has been all but forgotten. The United States signed—but did not ratify—the treaty.

Still, there are actions recommended by Jeffrey Sachs that could put us on the road to achieve these goals, including:

- removing subsidies to agriculture, fisheries, and energy production that harm the environment;
- introducing policies that encourage owners to manage property in ways that enhance ecosystem services;
- establishing protected habitats, like national parks, refuges, and marine areas within which fishing rights and commercial exploitation are curtailed;
- avoiding deforestation by giving carbon credits for keeping forests intact (to compensate for the income lost from cutting them down and selling the logs), as suggested by the Coalition of Rainforest Nations;
- improving agricultural productivity to reduce the need for arable land (more about this later);
- introducing sustainable food policies that incorporate the environmental cost of producing meat into the price of meat so that it accounts for the loss of biodiversity, feed grain production, pasture land, and excessive use of water (Such pricing policies together with consumer information should lead to a reduction in meat consumption worldwide.);
- protecting global fisheries by establishing tradable fishing quotas or permits, outlawing bottom trawling, and encouraging cultivating fish and other aquatic organisms rather than harvesting them from open waters; and
- limiting urban and suburban sprawl.

Jeffrey Sachs estimates, that preserving and somewhat restoring biodiversity would cost $35 billion annually, or 0.1 percent of the combined GDP of the rich countries.

In addition to preserving biodiversity, the most urgent task is securing water. Water stress is already causing severe problems. The greatest demand on water is from agriculture (70 percent). To provide water for agriculture, millions of wells were drilled to ever-increasing depths, pumping out groundwater that is not replenished anymore. Building dams is another way to divert and collect water, but this often deprives downstream populations. At any rate, the world's major river systems have already been dammed. The water shortage is further aggravated by pollution.

The United Nations Convention to Combat Desertification, adopted in 1992, recognized the need for global cooperation with respect to extreme water stress in the world's dry lands. The treaty has been mostly ignored by powerful nations. Much greater funding is required to confront the dry land crises in places like the Darfur region of Sudan, as well as Somalia and Ethiopia. The lack of water causes extreme poverty as well as conflict, which can end in war.

Regions most primed for water trouble are the Sahel, the Horn of Africa, Israel-Palestine, the Middle East, Pakistan, Central Asia, the Indo-Gangetic Plains, the North China Plain, the US Southwest, and the Murray-Darling Basin in Australia. Some areas for action (ref. 2) are discussed below.

First, let's consider the need to secure safe drinking water and sanitation for all. The Millennium Development Goals call for cutting in half the number of people without access to safe drinking water and sanitation. This is the easiest to achieve because it represents just a small part of the total water need. Engineering and financing are the elements missing here—not water resources. In 2006 the United Nations Development Plan (UNDP) estimated that the worldwide cost of meeting water and sanitation targets would be about $10 billion per year.

Another important action will be increasing water efficiency in agriculture through, for example, using drip-irrigation, low-till, or no-till systems (planting the seeds with minimal or no plowing) and developing drought-resistant seeds. The need to improve and increase the storage of rainwater in areas where rain and drought alternate is self-explanatory. Since we cannot treat water as free and limitless anymore we have to put a price on water, with subsidies for the poor and water tariffs for the rich.

Desalination of seawater is increasingly used in rich and oil-rich countries to create clean water. The various processes all require a lot of energy. While solar desalination may bring some hope to the near coastal areas of poor countries, the most water-stressed areas are far from coasts and often at higher altitudes where the transport of water consumes as much energy as the desalination process itself.

Climate change is increasing water stress immensely. Dry lands are becoming dryer, and wet areas will continue to get more floods and extreme events, while areas depending on annual snowmelt and long-term glacier melt will lose their water. The frequency and duration of droughts will rise significantly.

The population explosion from 1950 to now has magnified the water shortage, particularly since water-stressed regions had the largest population growth. Sub-Saharan Africa's population has more than quadrupled, from 180 million to 820 million, so too has the population of western Asia (including the Middle East).

Financial assistance for water management in low-income dry lands would require $35 billion annually from the developed donor countries, or 0.1 percent of their combined GDP (ref. 2).

– *Reducing world poverty*

The Millennium Development Goals (MDGs) are eight international development goals that 192 UN member states and at least twenty-three international organizations have agreed to achieve by the year 2015. The goals center around the reduction of poverty, hunger, disease, illiteracy, environmental degradation, and discrimination against women.

Forty-nine countries currently designated by the UN as "least developed countries" are not on track to meet the MDGs. The current criteria for being qualified as a least developed country are low national income (per capita GDP under $900), weak human assets (a composite index based on health, nutrition, and education indicators), and high economic vulnerability (a composite index based on indicators of instability of agricultural production and exports, inadequate diversification, and economic smallness).

The current populations of least developed countries (637 million people in total) are unable to achieve long-term growth and poverty reduction on their own and need help from developed countries. Since thirty-three of the forty-nine least developed countries are in Africa, we will discuss the help needed by their example.

These thirty-three African countries have the lowest agricultural yields in the world (as low as 0.5 ton of cereal per hectare). This is combined with the smallest farm sizes in the world (as small as 0.25 hectare per family, which is not enough to feed a family). Farm sizes can only decrease further because of the growing population and the lack of more arable land. Add to these factors the exhausted ecological systems and the increasing frequency and duration of droughts, and the result is people trapped in poverty and hunger.

In addition to widespread malnourishment, there are rampant diseases—HIV/AIDS, tuberculosis, malaria, and other infectious diseases—sapping productivity and ending lives prematurely. Mortality rates for children under age five are close to 18 percent, and the lifetime risk of dying in pregnancy or childbirth is one in thirteen in sub-Saharan Africa, a figure affected not only by maternal mortality but also by the great number of births per woman.

Illiteracy is widespread and even higher for women than men, further hampering the prospects of economic development. Infrastructure like roads, trains, ports, power grids, and water and sanitation systems are missing for a very large fraction of the population.

All these issues can be improved. Applying better technologies to agriculture—using high-yield seeds, fertilizer, proper planting techniques, and small-scale irrigation—can increase productivity. When productivity is raised above subsistence level, farmers can save, invest, and in time reach sustained growth.

The fight against diseases has made much progress. The Global Fund to Fight AIDS Tuberculosis and Malaria (started in 2001) has, as of 2007, funded the program in 132 countries, is treating over a million people suffering from AIDS with antiretroviral drugs as well as 2.8 million people with TB, and has distributed thirty million bed nets to protect against malaria. Private donors, such as the Gates Foundation, are funding research and development for drug and vaccine development as well as malaria control.

School attendance can be raised by providing free midday meals for pupils. Donating solar-powered laptops can increase education and connectivity.

Investment must be made in creating infrastructure to enable these countries to transport goods and become part of the global economy. Such investments, as important as they are for rural places, are even more important to urban areas; they have the potential to bring labor-intensive manufacturing jobs, for example, in the apparel and shoe industries, to these areas. Since Africa's manufacturing could and should be based on solar energy, replacing some of China's carbon-fuelled export industry would serve the environment as well as the development of African nations.

The concept of quick-impact investments that help to lift disadvantaged regions from extreme poverty was at the core of the recommendations by the UN Millennium Project directed by Jeffrey Sachs for former UN secretary-general Kofi Annan.

The Millennium Village Project was born to implement the Millennium Development Goals. The five-year effort aims to spend approximately $120 per villager per year (of which sixty dollars should come from external donors) in a community of about five thousand people. In total, about four hundred thousand people in seventy-eight villages were part of the project as of the end of 2006.

"Five goals were set for each village in the first year: a good harvest using improved inputs (high-yield seed and fertilizers); malaria control based on bed nets and medicines; clinical health services including the construction of new facilities if necessary; improved water sources for household use; improved attendance of children at school supported by a midday feeding program (using locally produced food if possible). The goals are quantified, budgeted and evaluated. The initial results have been very positive." (ref. 2)

These successes encouraged host governments to look toward scaling up the Millennium Village Project, partly by increasing the size of existing villages and also by introducing them in more districts throughout each country. Thus the Millennium Village Project scaled up, and combined with other initiatives on agriculture, health, education, and infrastructure, can make the difference in achieving the Millennium Development Goals.

But how is this all to be paid for? The commitments made in Gleneagles, Scotland, in 2005 and at every G8 meeting since stress the urgent need for action to invest in public services and social capital that will allow more than a billion people to escape poverty and make progress to achieve the MDGs. In 2005 the G8 meeting in Gleneagles raised the annual $25 billion contribution to $50 billion by 2010. The UN wants this to increase to 0.7 percent of the GDP of the wealthiest countries by 2013 in order to reach the MDGs by 2015.

The current GDP of the richest countries adds up to $35 trillion; 0.7 percent of this is $245 billion. This level of donation will be required yearly until the least developed countries reach self-sustaining growth and graduate from aid. How long aid will be needed depends on the yearly growth of their GDPs. Most rich countries are behind the timetable to fulfill their promise of aid. While 0.7 percent is a small fraction of a nation's GDP, it is a much larger fraction of each national government's budget; however, for the security of the world, this must become a priority.

– *Stabilizing the world's population*

Women who do not use contraception may give birth to six to nine children on average during their reproductive years; the probability

33

of becoming pregnant from unprotected sex is very high. Today fewer than one in seven sub-Saharan African women use any modern contraception. This results in very high total fertility rates (TFRs). As mentioned previously, TFR is the average number of children born to women during their reproductive years. Below are a few examples from the United Nations World Population Prospects 2006 Revision for the period between 2005 and 2010, along with data on the sizes of the relevant populations and their per capita GDPs.

country	TFR	per capita GDP in $	population million
Niger	7.19	896	12
Dem. Rep. of the Congo	6.70	675	65.7
Somalia	6.04	600	9.5
Rwanda	5.92	1431	10
Nigeria	5.32	1188	135
Ethiopia	5.29	859	83.7

Four of these countries qualify as "least developed countries," characterized by extreme poverty, hunger, disease, illiteracy, unemployment, and economic stagnation. Kenya, Niger, Tanzania, and Uganda, among others, have all more than quintupled in population since 1950. The two largest countries in sub-Saharan Africa, Nigeria and Ethiopia, have each more than quadrupled in population since 1950.

Poor families cannot improve their lots without a decline in fertility rates. They cannot feed, educate, and provide health care for so many children. As a result, the children face even more extreme poverty.

The countries themselves are very poor, unable to provide infrastructure, clinics, or schools for such rapidly increasing populations, let alone improve their citizens' lots in life. Not even a rich, developed country could provide services for a population that multiplies so rapidly.

We discussed already the effect of population growth on the environment and on climate change. There are other consequences too. Population growth greatly contributes to conflicts among starving and water-deprived communities; Somalia and Rwanda are just two of the examples. Another problem that rapid population growth creates is the resulting youth bulge. There are too many young, unemployed men, relative to older ones, prone to violence and wars and prey for recruiters of terrorist organizations. Afghanistan, for example, has a TFR of 7.07.

Nothing reduces TFR effectively, only the sustained use of modern contraceptives. Researchers working in Sub-Saharan Africa found that women do want to avoid unwanted pregnancies and be in control of how many children they have and how far apart they are born. They want more for their children, not more children, as described in historical context by Robert Engelmann (ref. 3), and indeed they wish to have access to modern contraceptives. But information, family planning services, clinics, and contraceptives are unavailable to them, mainly due to their poverty.

If TFRs remain as they are, the world's population will be 11.8 billion people by 2050, an amount that Earth cannot sustain.

It is important to note, that the greatest population increases take place in countries where a large population is combined with a large TFR, for example, in Nigeria and Ethiopia. But when a country has an extremely large population, like India (with a population of 1.15 billion in 2008), even with a TFR of 2.72, or a population growth rate of 1.55 percent, India's population would double in 45 years. Due to early marriage, on the average at age nineteen for women (in some regions as early as at age sixteen), and with the first child usually arriving in the first year of marriage, India's population growth, if its current TFR is not lowered fast, will have severe consequences for India and for Earth itself.

Some people argue that economic development itself will bring down TFRs. But this will not be the case if it is not coupled with educational and cultural development that results in the use of modern contraceptives. In Northern and Western Europe seven out of ten women use modern methods of contraception (in addition to some men using contraception). The above argument goes in the other direction. High fertility contributes directly to poor health, low levels of education, and high unemployment and thus to low national productivity, economic growth, and development. Economic development will happen after TFRs go down (see the modern development of Japan, China, South Korea and so on).

Some other people argue that once infant mortality rates go down, TFRs will go down too. But by what means? If parents are familiar with modern contraception and it is available to them, will they decide to have six children, because one of them may die (assuming a 16 percent infant mortality rate), and end up with five children, when they really wanted just two?

While everything possible must be done to reduce infant and maternal mortality rates, when mothers begin to have fewer children, spaced further apart, childcare will improve, and this in itself will significantly reduce infant and maternal mortality rates.

It is important that family planning programs are coupled with reproductive health services and prenatal and postnatal care for infants and mothers, as well as services for the prevention of sexually transmitted diseases including HIV/AIDS.

The most favored methods of contraception are the long-lasting methods and the permanent methods. Choosing a permanent method, such as female sterilization or male vasectomy, is a hard decision to make and is probably made only when the family's reproduction is already well above the replacement fertility rate. The long methods should be recommended instead.

Long-lasting methods include implants and intrauterine devices (IUDs or IUCDs). Copper-containing IUDs are effective up to twelve years; the initial cost is about $250, but they provide many years of protection. Progestin-containing subdermal implants last three to five years depending on type. USAID entered into a five-year procurement contract with Schering Oy for the provision of Jadelle at a cost of twenty-one dollars per set. (Roy Jacobstein, MD, MPH, clinical director of the Respond project, managed by EngenderHealth, a leading international reproductive health organization.)

Both long-acting methods are clinical methods and must be provided in health facilities by trained doctors, nurses, or midwives. Long-acting methods are by far the most effective (1 percent or less failure rate) and are safe and convenient. When they are removed, the return to fertility is quick. They do not protect against HIV/AIDS, and potential exposure to these and other sexually transmitted diseases requires the use of condoms, which unfortunately have a failure rate of 12 percent.

For any family planning and reproductive health care program to succeed, certain elements must be in place. Strong government commitment is required. Experiments show that, without strong and active government support, population programs falter. In Africa, like in many developing countries, the most successful programs are those that have strong government support. This is particularly important in rural areas, because authority plays an important role in the lives of rural people. The opinions of local administrators and community leaders can change traditional reproductive behavior.

Many governments, however, fail to achieve their population goals. For example in 2000 in India, the National Population Policy targeted reaching a TFR of 2.1 (the replacement fertility rate) by 2010. Instead the TFR will be 2.7 in 2010, while the population of India grew between 2000 and 2009 by 152 million people, more than the entire population of Russia (142 million).

Another critical element is a stronger role for the UN. The UN is the key to setting and implementing population goals. Reproductive rights were clarified and endorsed internationally in the Cairo Consensus that emerged from the 1994 International Conference on Population and Development (ICPD), which produced the following program of action:

Attaining the goals of sustainable, equitable development requires that individuals are able to exercise control over their sexual and reproductive lives. This includes rights to:

- reproductive health as a component of overall health, throughout the life cycle, for both men and women;
- reproductive decision making, including voluntary choice of marriage, family formation and *determination of the number* [emphasis added], timing and spacing of one's children and the right to have access to the information and means needed to exercise voluntary choice;
- equality and equity for men and women, to enable individuals to make free and informed choices in all spheres of life, free from discrimination based on gender; and
- sexual and reproductive security, including freedom from sexual violence and coercion and the right to privacy.

This author could not agree more with these goals, except for the reference to "determination of the number" of one's children, which contradicts current population goals and needs to be updated. The right to determine the number of children should be exchanged for the guarantee that "every woman independent of race, religion, and economic status has the right to have two healthy children."

This right is not enforceable; but the goal is to put pressure on governments to take their population goals seriously. Otherwise Africa will self-destruct, and India's population will march toward the two billion mark. It does not give license for governments to engage in coercion, forced sterilization or vasectomy, or the termination of pregnancies.

The work ahead looms large. It requires information, teaching, the establishment of health facilities, the training of doctors, nurses, midwives, the availability of long-acting contraceptives, and the training of community workers who visit homes, give information, and dispense temporary contraceptives.

Extremely important is the (at least) primary education of women and the support of their rights, as well as educating men to be partners to their wives.

Funding is another necessary factor. The UN Population Fund (UNFPA) is the lead agency in implementing the ICPD's program of action and the largest international source of funding for population and reproductive health programs. UNFPA made estimates in 1994 of what funds would be required in 2000 to reach the ICPD goals.

Purpose	$ billion
family planning programs	10.2
reproductive health services	5.0
prevention of sexually transmitted diseases including HIV/AIDS	1.3
population data collection, analysis, research	0.6
	17.1

Not even a tenth of these funds, were ever available to UNFPA. (The total contribution of donor countries in 2007 was $457.1 million.) Updating $17.1 billion to 2010 dollars amounts to $22.2 billion. Taking into account the enormous increase in reproductive age populations, to expand the program to more countries, would increase the size of the required funds to roughly 0.1 percent of the GDPs of donor countries ($35 trillion), or to $35 billion per annum.

This amount is expected to decrease and diminish in subsequent years when health facilities are in place, long-lasting contraceptives are supplied to a large fraction of women of reproductive age, and developing countries reach their Millennium Development Goals.

While the United States helped to establish UNFPA in 1969, played a leadership role in it, and until 1985 was the largest donor, providing nearly one-third of total annual funding, in recent years it has become an unreliable source of financial support. For fiscal year 2002, Congress allocated $34 million for UNFPA; however the Bush administration denied this approved funding for the last six fiscal years. In 2009 the US State Department resumed contributions to UNFPA and will contribute $50 million in 2009 and $60 million in 2010.

Of the US GDP ($14.2 trillion), only 0.1 percent ($14.2 billion) would need to be contributed annually to UNPFA. US military expenditures for 2010 are $626 billion. There is no doubt that population stabilization would do more to promote stability in the world than wars will. The US government needs to realize that failing nations become a threat to the world and to the United States and should spend its money accordingly. (Private persons can also make tax-deductible donations to UNFPA.)

The TFRs for Sub-Saharan African nations for the period between 2005 and 2010, shown in the table, were taken from the UN World Population Prospects 2006 Revision based on the medium fertility forecast. In the medium fertility forecast, the world's population will reach 9.2 billion by 2050. Realization of the medium variant in the 2006 Revision is contingent on ensuring that fertility continues to decline in developing countries. Fertility in the less developed countries as a whole is expected to drop from 2.75 children per woman (the figure between 2005 and 2010) to 2.05 children per woman between 2045 and 2050. The reduction expected in the fifty least developed countries is from 4.63 children per woman (2005–2010) to 2.50 children per woman (2045–2050). To achieve such a reduction it is essential that access to family planning expands to the poorest countries of the world.

But even this medium fertility forecast is not affordable. It means that the world's population will increase by 2.5 billion people, with most of this increase occurring in the poorest countries, where one billion people already do not have enough food. Who will feed them?

Even the low fertility forecast, where the fertility path is half a child below the medium variant, would lead to a population of 7.8 billion by mid-century. That is, at the world level, continued population growth until 2050 is inevitable (because of population momentum) even if the decline in fertility accelerates. A population of 7.8 billion in 2050 is still 1.1 billion people more than there are today, and that is the most we can possibly afford.

In summary, the Millennium Development Goals require 0.7 percent, biodiversity conservation, 0.1 percent, combating desertification, 0.1 percent, population stabilization, and reproductive health services, 0.1 percent, totaling 1.0 percent of the GDP of developed countries, or $350 billion per year. This does not include the amount, comparable in magnitude, that needs to be spent annually to mitigate climate change; this will have to come from a carbon tax.

The United States

– *Climate change*

Because per capita carbon emissions are highest in the United States, we in America will have to make the greatest per capita change. Recall that we have to reduce the per capita carbon emissions from the current 5.44 tons per year to 0.355 ton per year by mid-century. This requires large investments now. Furthermore, turning the situation around now would thwart the efforts by China and India to use US emissions as an excuse for refusing to commit to legally binding reductions in greenhouse gas emissions.

The government will have to spend about 1 percent of the US GDP, or $140 billion per year, to invest in carbon-reducing technologies. How else can the US government raise money than by taxes? The most straightforward method is to have a carbon tax and spend it on reducing carbon emissions in the most efficient and transparent ways. How else will we change our wasteful ways, if it does not cost us money? Cap and trade could easily be used for profit rather than to reduce the carbon content of the atmosphere.

If we do not act, it does not mean that life will go on as before. Climate change is not free. The total damage from Hurricane Katrina, in which 1,836 people died, was about $100 billion and counting. What if there were a Katrina every year? What if there were larger hurricanes—and more than one per year? And what are the costs of forest fires, droughts, and floods in human lives and in property and crop damage? Climate change surely will cost more than its mitigation.

Part of a carbon tax should be spent on carbon capture and storage (CCS): carbon capture deployment on a commercial scale at the point of source, such as in coal-fired power plants, as well as from the ambient.

Deforestation, forest degradation and forest fires account for about 20 percent of worldwide greenhouse gas emissions; thus halting forest loss is one of the most cost-effective ways to mitigate climate change.

Another important method is regenerative farming (using compost, manure, or cover crops); this captures greenhouse gases from the ambient and stores it in the form of carbon in the ground, improving soil quality and water retention as well.

The carbon dioxide that is produced as agricultural waste, dead trees, and so on decompose can be captured and stored instead, using modern biochar technology, which uses pyrolysis to heat biomass in the absence of oxygen, turning it to biochar, a form of charcoal. The substance can be buried in the soil, thereby improving soil quality and water retention.

Part of the carbon tax should be spent on a modernized national power grid, increasing safety and enabling the inclusion of carbon-free (and thus carbon tax-free) energy. The national smart grid would cost an estimated $400 billion over ten years; both private sector and federal investment will be required.

Additionally it will be important to enable the construction of modern nuclear fission power plants, particularly in states where all power comes from coal; to pursue research and development to accelerate nuclear fusion technologies; and last but not least, to educate the public about these issues so that resistance is not based on ignorance or outdated information. The table below demonstrates how a federal carbon tax could be spent.

10 percent: commercial-scale carbon capture and storage at typical, existing coal-fired power plants to demonstrate feasibility and economy; to accelerate the implementation of black carbon emission regulations, including maritime shipping

20 percent: afforestation, reforestation, improved forest management, improved forest fire prevention, protection of primary growth forests; subsidies for regenerative farming and large-scale application of biochar technologies

10 percent: support for international efforts to reduce emissions from deforestation and forest degradation in developing countries by providing financial incentives on a global scale to conserve forests rather than convert them; aid black carbon reduction projects in developing countries, including the distribution of solar and/or more efficient cook stoves (one hundred million pieces)

20 percent: renewal of the existing electric power grid to a HVDC (high-voltage direct-current) one, including storage points and "smart" features enabling inclusion of electricity from alternate sources, more efficient transport, and usage

10 percent: new HVDC power grids to wind and solar energy farms in the American Midwest and Southwest to make these energies competitive with fossil fuel energy

20 percent: encouragement of new nuclear fission power plant construction in large numbers; expansion and extension of the

nuclear production tax credit; provision of loan guaranties for new plants; enhancement of other incentives

5 percent: dramatic increase of monetary and intellectual investment in nuclear fusion energy development to speed up ITER, laser-ignited fusion or other schemes

5 percent: high-level education of policy makers and industry leaders; science-based energy education of the public using the media in addition to educational facilities

How much will it cost? We will estimate the two easiest examples: the magnitude of a carbon tax on electricity and on gasoline. We take the peer-reviewed price of forty-three dollars per metric ton of carbon dioxide (the price of a ton of carbon is 3.666 times more, $157.6). The national average of carbon dioxide emissions upon generating one kilowatt-hour of electricity is 0.618 kilogram (where coal-fired power plants represent 44.4 percent; natural gas-fired power plants, 23.2 percent; nuclear power plants, 20.4 percent; hydroelectric, 7.1 percent; renewables, 3.6 percent; petroleum liquids, 1.1 percent). If the price of 1 kilogram carbon dioxide is 4.3 cents (4,300/1,000), that of 0.618 kilogram is 2.7 cents.

Taking the monthly average electricity consumption in the United States as 936 kilowatt-hours, the monthly electric bill would increase by twenty-five dollars or about 30 percent, if the electricity price is 9.13 cents per kilowatt-hour.

Because of the way the energy industry is regulated in the United States, consumer prices will go up much more slowly than in unregulated markets, taking many years to materialize. If a greater percentage of electricity comes from nuclear, hydro, and renewable energy sources, the tax will become less. After all, the purpose of the carbon tax is to eliminate itself.

With the smart grid, electricity prices will go down due to lower transportation costs. The smart grid will also enable the use of cheaper electricity (off-peak hours). Last, but not least, driving energy savings by encouraging better insulation and more efficient appliances, and so on, is at the heart of the carbon tax. About 70 percent of the population could likely afford such a tax; the remaining 30 percent would receive their carbon tax expenditures back as tax rebates.

Let us now estimate the carbon tax on gasoline. One gallon of gasoline emits 8.9 kilograms of carbon dioxide; taking again the price of 1 kilogram of carbon dioxide as 4.3 cents gives 38 cents of carbon tax on a gallon of gasoline. At the time of this writing the average price of a gallon of gasoline was $2.67; this includes 18.4 cents federal tax. With the mean value of the state tax being 27.2 cents, the sum of 45.6 cents tax per gallon of gasoline is currently included in the price. The carbon tax would be added to this.

In the European Union, the gasoline price is five to six dollars per gallon, depending on the country, or roughly twice the price of gas in the United States. While in the United States fuel taxes are often dedicated to highway projects, giving the impression of a "user's fee," in other countries the fuel tax is a source of general revenue. Many European countries, such as the UK, France, and Italy use the fuel tax to decrease dependence on fossil fuels, reduce traffic, and reduce pollution.

It is said that Americans are addicted to oil. The truth is that they are addicted to the personal automobile, primarily because of the need to commute long distances from suburban homes to workplaces.

– *Housing*

Promoting home ownership started as a government policy during the Great Depression and has had an ever increasing role since, by such methods as giving mortgage assistance in 1944 to returning veterans, extending mortgages to minorities in the 1960s and 1970s, and so on. Direct or indirect government sponsorship of mortgage debt through Freddie Mac (Federal Home Loan Corporation) and Fannie Mae (Federal National Mortgage Association) and the existence of the Federal Loan Banks fund pushed mortgages to lower interest rates and longer terms, requiring smaller and smaller down payments and extended them to riskier borrowers.

Over the course of those decades many people owned their homes because of government programs, which also created suburban sprawl, gutted inner cities, and caused long commutes.

In the 1990s and 2000s the government's promotion of home ownership further accelerated.

The securitization of mortgages and subprime lending changed the act of buying a home into an investment, with endless returns on down payments of just a few percent, and a cash cow, when borrowing against the value of the home (home equity loans) could be used to finance personal consumption.

Because government policies unleashed enormous amounts of capital, single-family house construction and real estate became critical economic sectors, and new housing starts became a leading indicator of the country's economic health. Housing wealth (including mortgages) totaled $13 trillion at its peak in 2006, almost as large as the GDP.

Is this good for the economy? Government-sponsored home ownership favors investments in real estate instead of factories, equipment, businesses, new ventures, and so on. Roughly half of the price of a single family house pays for the land it stays on. This half of the price does not create jobs, while the other half creates jobs only while the house is being built. A house should last for a hundred years (at least), during which time period it does not create jobs, and the money that is bound up in home mortgages is not being lent to businesses.

Of course, people have to live somewhere, but this could be accomplished more modestly. The 2007 American Housing Survey showed that the median amount of space per person is 769 square feet. Fair enough for a single person living alone, but is 3,076 square feet really required for a family of four?

Smaller living spaces—and, yes, apartments—are more economical, impart greater mobility to pursue better employment, leave more free time and more savings to invest in businesses (and thus create jobs). For the US economy to depend that much on housing construction, the population has to grow constantly, which is something we cannot afford anymore.

Then came the economic crisis. Because government policies promoted mortgage borrowing and lending, the government arguably contributed to the subprime mortgage crisis. Many innocent people lost their jobs, and the federal government paid a price on the order of a trillion dollars, increasing its indebtedness to unsustainable levels.

A further government subsidy to home owners is the tax deductibility of the mortgage interest. How did this start? A notice in the 1913 federal tax code allowed for deduction of home mortgage interest payments. The reason was that for small proprietors (like the storeowner whose business was on street level and whose family lived above) it was difficult to separate business and personal expenses, so it was simpler to allow the deduction of all interest. But those times were very different; workers built their houses themselves, and the rich paid full. Having a debt was considered a shame. Mortgages were for a maximum of 50 percent of the home price and had to be repaid in three to five years.

This tax subsidy costs the federal government an estimated $80 to 100 billion annually in lost revenue, an amount sorely needed to reduce the budget deficit.

IRS data show that the bulk of mortgage interest deductions are claimed by upper-income taxpayers and few low- and middle-income families (many of whom do not even itemize deductions), which encourages larger and more expensive homes among a relatively small group of taxpayers rather than promoting broad-based home ownership among ordinary Americans. Nothing proves this better than the fact that the percentage of homeowners in Canada and the UK, where mortgage interest is not deductible, is the same (68 percent) as in the United States, where the mortgage interest is tax-deductible. And how about the justice (the *in*justice) of allowing the deduction of interest on home equity loans used for personal consumption?

In the interest of establishing a level playing field for owners and renters, benefiting the economy, and reducing government debt, the tax deductions for home mortgage interest should be phased out.

Let's examine the effect of homeownership on climate change. A suburban homeowner commuting twenty-three miles a day with a twenty-three-mile-per-gallon car for 332 days a year puts about three tons of carbon dioxide (332 × 0.009) annually into the air to stay there for two hundred years. Three tons of carbon dioxide is equivalent to 0.818 ton of carbon. Our total yearly allowance should be 0.355 ton of carbon, less than what is contributed by the commuting alone. This is how serious the situation is.

The American Dream is *not* about owning a house with a three-car garage in the suburbs. The American Dream is about having the freedom and opportunity to bring out the best of one's talents for the benefit of oneself and one's children, community, nation, and world.

– *Immigration*

The law. The Immigration and Nationality Act (INA) of 1952 consolidated previous immigration laws. It established a 150,000 persons per year limit on immigration from the Eastern Hemisphere, giving preference to those ethnicities that already made up the population of the United States (predominantly from Western and Northern Europe), using the "national origins" formula, based on the ethnic background of the entire US population, as revealed by the 1920 census. Within the quota system, first preference was given to those whose skills were needed by the US economy; persons with family relations to US citizens or permanent residents received lower preferences (spouses, minor children, and parents of US citizens were not subject to the quota system).

The 1965 amendments replaced the national origins formula, considered discriminatory against Eastern and Southern Europeans, with a limit of twenty thousand from each country in the Eastern Hemisphere and an overall limit of 170,000 for that hemisphere. The law established a quota of 120,000 for the Western hemisphere without limits for any particular countries.

While President Kennedy wanted skill-based immigration considerations, President Johnson gave priority to family unification. Allegedly President Johnson wanted to reward US citizens of Eastern and Southern European ethnicity (considered loyal Democrats) to be able to bring relatives to the United States. The existence of the Iron Curtain made this impossible, and immigrants from the Western Hemisphere took their place.

While over two-thirds of the legal immigrants admitted during the 1950s originated in Europe or Canada, 25 percent in Latin America, and 6 percent in Asia, by the 1990s only 16 percent originated in Europe or Canada, while 49 percent hailed from Latin America and 32 percent from Asia (ref.4).

According to the Migration Policy Institute's 2007 study, the top ten immigrant-sending countries in 2006 were in decreasing order: Mexico, China, Philippines, India, Cuba, Colombia, Dominican Republic, El Salvador, Vietnam, and Jamaica.

The primary goal of the current immigration policy has remained family unification. While there is no limit on the immigration of immediate relatives (spouses, minor children, parents) of US citizens, other immigrants are subject to numerical limitations separated into preference categories (ref. 5):

a. Family-sponsored preferences permit the immigration of 480,000 relatives in four categories. Immediate relatives, who immigrated the year before, are deducted from this number, but the 1990 Act mandates that the family-sponsored immigration quota must be at 226,000. Family-sponsored preferences are subdivided into four groups:

First preference: unmarried adult sons and daughters of US citizens.

Second preference: spouses, children, and unmarried sons and daughters of permanent resident aliens.

Third preference: married sons and daughters of US citizens.

Fourth preference: brothers and sisters of US citizens. Since immigration by immediate relatives is unlimited, the overall number of persons immigrating due to family relationships is far more than 480,000 per year, and it increases every year.

b. Employment-related preferences: The quota for this category is 140,000 immigrants per year, divided into five categories:

First preference: priority workers, such as persons of extraordinary ability, outstanding professors and researchers, multinational executives and managers.

Second preference: professionals holding advanced degrees, or persons of exceptional ability in the sciences, arts, or business.

Third preference: skilled workers in short supply, professionals holding baccalaureate degrees.

Fourth preference: certain special immigrants, such as religious workers and former employees of the US government and international organizations.

Fifth preference: employment creation. This preference category is for investors who will create jobs investing in a new enterprise benefiting the economy.

c. Diversity immigrants: 55,000 people, who are neither family-sponsored nor employment preferred, are selected by a lottery from areas that have low representation in sending immigrants to the United States.

d. Inhabitants of Hong Kong and other special groups: Due to the return of Hong Kong to the People's Republic of China, the per-country immigration limit for Hong Kong is the same (twenty thousand) as for an independent state. (There is a per-country limit of twenty thousand on immigration that does not count immigration by immediate relatives. Because of the great backlog in second-preference, family-sponsored immigration from certain countries, particularly from Mexico, the 1990 Act exempted 75 percent of the second-preference limitation from the per-country limits.)

– *The impact of immigration laws*

In this author's view the 1965 amendments were not well thought-out. They reflected the needs of peasant societies of long ago, not the situations and requirements of our times. Family unification parameters allow for much more than what is even possible for natives themselves. How many adult Americans live near their siblings, married children, or even parents and in-laws? Immigration does not mean bringing your entire old environment with you; it means starting a new life and new relationships. To bring a large family, which needs support, prevents risk-taking, which is surely needed in establishing a new life, and it prevents assimilation in the new country.

Most important, *the result of the 1965 amendments has been that the US government has lost control over the quality and the quantity of immigrants.* The family-sponsored law means that the immigrants—not the US government—decide who the next immigrants will be.

A large proportion of the immigrants who entered the United States after 1965 came from developing nations, and this group is significantly less skilled than previous immigrants. While immigrants from the UK, as of 1990, had an average of 14.6 years of schooling, those from Mexico had only 7.6 years, not even the equivalent of graduating from middle school.

It makes a great difference whether an immigrant comes from the top 25 percent of the workforce of a developed country or from the bottom 10 percent of the workforce of a developing country.

Of the some twenty Nobel prizes in physics awarded to immigrants in the twentieth century and beyond, fifteen were awarded to scientists who came from developed countries, highly educated and already prominent in their fields: four came from China (two were educated in developed countries from primary school on) and one, from India (and was also educated in a developed country).

The one who had the greatest influence on the fate of the United States by creating the first artificial self-sustaining nuclear chain reaction, Italian Enrico Fermi, came with the 1938 Nobel Prize in Physics in his pocket.

These people were outstanding not because they were immigrants but because they were highly educated and came from highly educated countries. As Louis Pasteur said in 1853, "Chance favors the mind which is prepared."

The percent of high school dropouts among immigrant men as of 1998 is 33.6 percent, compared to 9.0 percent of native men. Because of the lack of education, the poverty rate of Mexican immigrants is 33 percent. This does not deter the import of more poor immigrants. If the sponsor's household income exceeds 125 percent of the poverty line (if his own family consists of four persons, the poverty line is $22,050; 125 percent of this is $27,562) he can sponsor the entry of two additional relatives.

Because these immigrants are less educated and have larger families, with more children and older people in their households, there is a welfare gap between immigrants and natives.

Immigrant participation in welfare started to rise after 1965, and now they receive a disproportionately large share of welfare benefits. By the late 1990s almost a quarter of immigrant households received assistance compared to 15 percent of native households. There are large differences in the percentages of immigrant households on welfare according to their countries of origin. A quarter of immigrants originating in El Salvador or Nigeria receive benefits, along with a third originating in Cuba and Mexico, and close to 60 percent coming from the Dominican Republic or Laos, indicating that country of origin matters (ref. 4).

In California, which receives almost 60 percent of Mexican immigrants to the United States and has the most generous welfare benefits, the National Academy of Sciences determined that immigration increased the state and local taxes of the typical native household by $1,174 annually.

Many unskilled immigrants do not bother or are unable to learn enough English to advance in the American economy. This is furthered by clustering in a few big cities, such as Mexicans in the barrios of East Los Angeles and Cubans in Miami's Little Havana (ref. 4). Immigrants who live in ethnic enclaves can get by without proficiency in English and without changing. Advancing in the American workplace requires mastering the English language, being dynamic, moving to places where economic advantage appears, learning in general, and learning new skills.

An immigrant cannot have it both ways; he or she cannot keep the language, habits, expertise (or lack thereof), productivity, and work culture of the old country, but get paid more for it.

Most important, nothing influences the future labor market performance of children more than the education levels of their parents. But even if parents are not well educated, if they instill in their children an understanding of the value of learning, the children will learn.

Overall only just over a tenth of Hispanics or Latinos have a four-year college degree (as compared to about a third of non-Hispanic whites, 17 percent of non Hispanic blacks, and almost half of Asian Americans). Others go to community colleges or join the armed services, but the majority eventually move into the same low-skilled jobs as their parents (ref. 4).

The number of legal immigrants to the United States is at its highest level ever: 37.5 million. This, of course, is the result of family-sponsored immigration preference. Let's assume one immigrant brings his wife and two minor children; both he and his wife can bring two parents, and each can bring siblings, who in turn can bring wives and children. By assuming just two siblings for the husband and two for the wife, and not more than two children for each, one immigrant can bring in twenty-three relatives (family chain migration). Did anyone in the government make a numerical estimate of where the 1965 Act might lead? In addition to the 37.5 million legal immigrants in the United States, there are an estimated twelve million illegal immigrants in the country. The populations of both legal and illegal immigrants increase by over one million people each per year.

Further contributing to the population explosion is the fact that the total fertility rate of immigrants, in particular Hispanics, is greater than the replacement fertility rate. The TFR of non-Hispanic whites is 2.0, of non-Hispanic blacks 2.2, where their weighted average gives the ideal replacement fertility rate (between 2.0 and 2.1). Hispanic women have the unsustainable fertility rate of 3.0; among immigrant women from Mexico, the rate is 3.5. Since women's overall level of education is a good predictor of fertility rates, the high percentage of immigrant women without a high school diploma probably explains the fertility rate difference between Hispanic women and native women as well as the difference in teen pregnancy rates (2.6 percent for non-Hispanic whites, 6.2 percent for non-Hispanic blacks, and 8.2 percent for Hispanics).

As a consequence of this immigration and the TFR of immigrant groups, the population of the United States, which was 194 million in 1965 is now about 308 million giving the United States the highest population growth rate among developed nations—a non-sustainable rate. If the current trend continues, the population of the United States is predicted to be 420 million (or, according to Census Bureau estimates, 439 million) by 2050 with the following racial composition change:

	2008	2050
non-Hispanic whites	66 percent	46 percent
Hispanics	15 percent	30 percent
non Hispanic blacks	14 percent	15 percent
Asian Americans	5 percent	9 percent

Of the nation's children, only 38 percent will be non-Hispanic whites in 2050.

The economic benefit from immigration is small, estimated by George Borjas and other researchers to be around $10 billion annually, which, in a $14 trillion economy, is miniscule. Apart from the $25 billion (approximate) revenue sent back to their countries of origin by immigrants, the $10 billion benefit counts against the cost of welfare programs, public services, and externalities to be discussed later.

Because the majority of recent immigrants are unskilled workers, they depress the wages in the low-earning categories; low-skilled native workers lose income; their loss appears as gain to the employers of immigrants and those who use immigrant services. Immigration to the United States redistributes—rather than creates—wealth, as shown by George Borjas in *Heaven's Door*. It increases the income gap between unskilled and skilled workers and counteracts US social policies that are intended to improve the economic condition of low-wage earners.

The often-used one-liner—"Immigrants take jobs, that natives do not want"—does not have much truth to it. Natives are represented in great numbers in all job categories in which immigrants work. Natives want to earn fair wages at these jobs and do not want to be exploited; they are Americans.

It should be noted that at the time of this writing the unemployment rate in Mexico is 5.3 percent, while the rate in the United States is about 10 percent (much higher if those who are underemployed or have given up looking for jobs are added), and, most sadly, the unemployment rate of native black men between ages sixteen and nineteen is 57 percent!

Most interesting are the numbers for agriculture. Agriculture, forestry and fishing employ less than one million laborers, 0.6 percent of the US workforce of 153.1 million (this figure includes the unemployed). Out of this, one out of eight jobs, or about 114,000, are filled by workers from Mexico. There are 3.8 million Mexicans in California, where much of our handpicked produce is grown, yet the majority of produce sold in California's supermarkets is imported from Mexico; furthermore our trade deficit with Mexico was $47.5 billion for 2009.

The labor need of agriculture certainly does not justify the presence of 37.5 million legal and more than twelve million illegal immigrants, totaling about fifty million people. Cheap labor prevents investment in new technology, like fruit-picking robot systems, where investment and development should be focused, ultimately providing the United States with less expensive and more reliable labor as well as a potential export industry.

The great wave of immigration unleashed by the 1965 Immigration Act disproportionately increased the supply of unskilled workers and decreased the percentage of skilled workers. The United States runs an increasing trade deficit by importing not only goods requiring the labor of low-skilled workers but also advanced technology products. Currently the United States imports $53 billion per year more in advanced technology products than it exports.

After a long hiatus, we urgently need to build nuclear power plants. Our nuclear power industry and our ability to design new reactors were lost many years ago. We must get back into this field. So many high-tech products that we pioneered (television, mobile phones, LCD, consumer electronics, and so on) were lost, along with their manufacturing infrastructure and employment. And many more of our current innovative industries are at risk, such as solid-state lighting using LEDs, thin-film solar cells, optical communication components, carbon composites for aerospace and wind-energy applications, flash memory chips, and more.

The old business model for the US economy—increasing the population, pouring more concrete, and selling more cars—will not work for the twenty-first century.

Our livelihood will have to come from a knowledge-based economy, and we have an undersupply of educated, independent-thinking, and innovative workers capable of handling new technologies and complex issues.

We have an oversupply of marginally skilled workers. But human capital is not the same as a piece of machinery; it cannot be discarded when obsolete. The US economy is stuck with unskilled immigrant workers, and most unfortunately, statistics show that the majority of their children remain at the same skill level, thus this will be with us for a long time to come.

In California non-Hispanic whites made up 80 percent of the population in 1970; this is now down to 43 percent. California was number one among the states in educational attainment. The underperformance of Latino students greatly contributed to the state becoming the forty-fifth among states.

California is the bellwether for the country as a whole. Over five million students in the United States, or more than one in ten of all enrolled in public schools, are English learners. It takes five to seven years for these students to write essays, understand a novel, or explain scientific processes at the level of their English-speaking classmates.

Many parents worried that the influx of Latino students strained the resources of schools and lowered the quality of their children's education. How can children learn when teachers have to spend most of their time with students who do not even understand what the teachers tell them?

The decline of American schools is well known. What is less known is that the quality of our science and math education was ranked forty-third among nations by the World Economic Forum Executive Opinion Survey 2006–2007.

Is immigration good for Latino children? Not necessarily so. Speaking from personal experience, it is very hard to learn subjects like biology or history in a language you do not know yet. It can rob you of confidence in your learning ability. Perhaps if these children had stayed in Mexico, they could have studied in their own language, became confident in their learning abilities, studied for more years, and advanced socially and economically more than they have been able to here.

Mexico is an upper-middle-income democracy; it has the eleventh largest economy in the world, predicted to become the fifth largest by 2050. It has the highest purchasing power parity in Latin America, is North America's largest automaker (surpassing the United States), and will have universal health care by 2011, again surpassing the United States.

Income inequality remains a problem. There are huge gaps between rich and poor, and those living in urban and rural areas. It is the duty of the Mexican government to solve this problem instead of letting—and possibly encouraging—their poorest to emigrate to the United States illegally.

We certainly have to help the children of uneducated immigrants who are here already. First, the mothers need to be educated so that they can take part in their children's education. They have to learn to be proficient in English, read to their children in English, and become involved with school and homework. They also have to be educated in and receive family planning services (as discussed in the chapter about population stabilization) so they will have children later in life and will not have more than the replacement fertility rate. They must not rob future generations of Americans from being able to have two children because of unsustainable population growth.

The United States will have to spend an immense amount of labor and money to help the children who are here already but should not allow more uneducated immigrants. If the current trend continues, it will further accelerate the decline of our schools.

Over 80 percent of the population growth in the United States is due to immigration and the high fertility rate of immigrant women. Is an increased population sustainable?

In the 1950s and 1960s, during the Green Revolution, agriculture became industrialized, increasing grain production by applying better seeds and making use of about fifty times more energy than the sun, human, and animal labor provide in traditional agriculture. All of this extra energy came from the fossil fuels required to make fertilizers, herbicides, and pesticides; operate field machinery; pump water for irrigation; and so on. In the United States four hundred gallons of oil equivalents are used annually to feed one American. Because the soil is increasingly eroded and lacks more and more nutrients, more and more fertilizer is needed to create the same crop yield. Because much grain is grown as monoculture, more and more pesticides are needed. More and more irrigation is required as there begins to be a serious water shortage in the Western United States. In *Food, Land, Population and the US Economy* published in 1994 by Mario Giampietro (Instituto Nazionale della Nutrizione, Rome) and David Pimentel (Cornell University) estimate that the maximum population of the United States for a sustainable agriculture is two hundred million people, provided we will have the necessary fossil fuels.

In 2007, 37.6 million Americans (of 308 million) were living in poverty, and many of them did not have enough food.

Our immigration policy does not give consideration to our less fortunate fellow Americans and our children and grandchildren.

It is known that immigrants settle mainly in big cities. If our immigration policy does not change, for example, in twenty years there will be between nine and eighteen million more Texans, according to the Texas state demographer's prediction. This will mainly increase the population of three of America's most populous cities, Houston, San Antonio and Dallas, along with Austin and Fort Worth. These metro areas are home now to thirteen million people creating large traffic jams. Add to these sprawling metroplexes many millions more. Do we want our cities to become like Mumbai, Mexico City, and New Delhi?

Do we have the money for infrastructure, education, police, hospitals, prisons, and roads? Spending increasing amounts of time in traffic jams will cost hundreds of billions of dollars in wasted fuel and time. Are we getting into this mess as a result of an informed decision or swept toward it by ignorance and complacency?

In addition, since immigrants come from low-consuming, low-energy-using, low-carbon-dioxide- emitting countries to the highest-consuming, highest energy-using and highest-carbon-emitting country in the world, this is going to have an adverse effect on climate change. US emissions increased in parallel with population. As mentioned earlier the annual per capita level of carbon emissions in the United States, as of 2007, was 5.44 tons. If the US population keeps growing at the current rate and per capita emissions remain the same, by 2050 the annual carbon emissions of the United States alone will be exceeding the global limit of 2.4 gigatons per year.

Illegal immigrants are estimated to be about twelve million people; 57 percent come from Mexico and 24 percent from other Latin American countries, primarily in Central America. Illegal immigrants are hired at lower wages than citizens and are employed in service jobs, construction, and so on, but only 3 to 4 percent of them work in agriculture. They depress the wages of low-income US citizens, particularly of African Americans.

The Congressional Budget Office found that the tax revenues illegal aliens generate for state and local governments do not offset the total cost of services provided to them, such as emergency room services and so on. The estimated cost of educating illegal alien students and citizen children of illegal aliens as of 2004 was $29.6 billion.

Sure, the companies who hire them profit, but the rest of us pay for this profit. Sure, the upper income households who hire them as gardeners, maids, and nannies profit, but school taxes go up two to three times for all others who do not profit from their cheap labor.

The US Department of Homeland Security criticized a program in the state of Yucatan, Mexico, and that of a federal Mexican agency that helped illegal immigrants get to the United States. The agency gave booklets of information about routes, where to find water and food, and so on, as well as advice to those who were here already in the United States about how to remain undetected, receive US-government-run social services, and send money back to Mexico.

It sure is good business for Mexico to get rid of their poorest and least educated, and in addition get $18 billion each year in revenue sent back home to them. But it is surely bad business for the United States.

In addition to the American government becoming serious about border protection (see H.R. 4437), the cooperation of the Mexican government is needed to cut down on illegal immigration; this should include "deep repatriation" by which apprehended immigrants are transported to cities in southern and central Mexico. (The Mexican government, not the US government, should pay for this.) It is easier to control "out-migration" from the country where they are documented than "in-migration" to a country where they are not.

Serious fines of thousands of dollars should be imposed on those who employ illegal aliens, and this money should be used for their humane repatriation.

Along with higher wages and the promise of welfare benefits, amnesty and birthright citizenship are magnets for illegal immigration.

The 1986 Immigration and Reform Control Act gave amnesty to 2.8 million aliens. This was supposed to be a *one-time-only* amnesty. Yet six different amnesties for illegal aliens have been passed by Congress since—Section 245(i) Amnesties, Nation Specific Amnesties NACARA Amnesty of 1997, HRIFA Amnesty of 1998, Late Amnesty of 2000, LIFE Act Amnesty of 2000—giving amnesty to another three million aliens, bringing the total of amnesty given to 5.8 million. In addition, becoming citizens entitled them to bring in large numbers of family members.

Currently illegal aliens number about twelve million. If they became citizens, each is entitled to bring in at least their immediate family members as legal immigrants. Spouse, children, parents, as a minimum 5 immediate family members. If they are not included in the twelve million, then amnesty for 12 million illegal immigrants means a commitment in time to about *seventy- two million* new legal immigrants-most of them poor and uneducated-and not selected by the United States government, but by law-breaking aliens.

It is obvious to everyone but Congress that amnesty encourages further illegal immigration. It rewards those who break the law and entices more to break the law.

The Fourteenth Amendment to the Constitution, adopted in 1868, declares that all persons born in the United States and subject to the jurisdiction thereof are citizens of the United States and of the state wherein they reside. The Citizenship Clause was intended to go further than the common law and include all African Americans born in the United States. Before the amendment, African Americans, whether enslaved or free people, had been denied the status of US citizenship by an 1857 Supreme Court declaration.

The Civil War led to the abolition of slavery; however, because of the 1857 Supreme Court decision, it was argued that while the Emancipation Proclamation had freed African Americans, they could not become citizens without a constitutional amendment, thus the Fourteenth Amendment was adopted.

Clearly, it has not been needed for some 140 years, but it is in effect and is used by illegal aliens and tourists.

Four hundred thousand babies per year are born in US hospitals at taxpayers expense to illegal immigrants, that is, 10 percent of all births. They are called "anchor babies" because as US citizens they become eligible to sponsor the legal immigration of their illegal alien parents and siblings, a minimum of 4 people, when they become twenty-one years of age. This means, that because of birthright citizenship the US is committed to *two million* new legal immigrants per year, not selected by the US government but by law-breaking aliens-most of them poor and uneducated. As a comparison our cap for employment-preferred immigration is 140 thousand people per year.

It takes more, than being born on American soil to become an American. It requires parents who instill in their children traditional American values, allegiance to their country, a sense of belonging to the culture, and knowledge of the language and history. Birthright citizenship is depreciating the value of US citizenship.

No European country except Romania grants birthright citizenship.

Canada is the only developed country other than the United States to grant birthright citizenship. But the Canadian population is only 34 million, and their southern neighbor is the United States.

Bills were introduced in Congress in 2005 (H.R. 698) and in 2007 (H.R. 1940) to declare that American-born children of illegal immigrants and tourists, thus foreign nationals, are not subject to the "jurisdiction" of the United States and are thus not entitled to citizenship via the Fourteenth Amendment, unless at least one parent is a US citizen or lawful permanent resident or serves in the armed forces. Neither of these, nor any similar bills, was approved by Congress.

Some legislators have proposed that the Citizenship Clause be changed through constitutional amendment. Senate Joint Resolution 6, introduced on January 16, 2009, proposes such an amendment; however, this has not been approved by Congress for ratification by the states, nor has any other similar proposed amendment.

But this has to happen as soon as possible because we are losing control over the nation's future. It is the American people and not law-breaking aliens who should determine the demographic future of the country.

"We are a nation of immigrants" is the knee-jerk reaction to any attempt at immigration reform. Every nation was a nation of immigrants at different times in history. We were a nation of slaveholders too. Times change.

We had a large wave of unskilled immigrants arrive at the end of the nineteenth century and the beginning of the twentieth, when industrialization required unskilled machine operators to mass-produce consumer goods inexpensively and make them available to a larger fraction of the population. Previously, these goods had been expensive because they were handmade by skilled artisans (and they continued to be handmade for the wealthy during that time). But when our need subsided, we almost completely closed the door to immigration in 1924.

Do not confuse immigration with humanitarian aid. Sure, poor immigrants make more money and get more welfare assistance if they come to the United States, where even reduced wages are higher than in their own countries, but the whole world makes less money than Americans (excepting the people of Qatar, Luxembourg, Norway, Brunei, and Singapore).

There are close to three billion people living in poverty in the world today. Do you want to bring them all to the United States? Instead give humanitarian aid to needy people in their own countries, where per capita GDP is less than $1,000, as discussed earlier.

Diversity immigration does not benefit the United States; it only adds to our unsustainable population growth (under current law, after becoming citizens these individuals can also bring large numbers of relatives into the country). Remember that we are not the United Nations but the United States of America; it is not more diversity we need now, but more unity. There is no proven relation between diversity and skills, only between education and skills.

In 2009 we had 1,130,818 legal immigrants plus 400,000 new birthright citizens adding up to 1,530,818 new legal immigrants (in addition to close to one million new illegal immigrants). We have an out-of-hand surge of mass immigration as a consequence of our immigration laws and the inability, or unwillingness to protect our borders.

We clearly need an immigration reform that results in the dramatic decrease of immigrants coming to our country. Out of the 1.5 million legal immigrants, the immediate relatives of US citizens (an untouchable immigration category) accounted for 535,554 persons in 2009. The number of legal immigrants accepted in any immigration category must be multiplied by about six, because of the right as US citizens to bring in as legal immigrants their immediate family. The number of immigrants in the immediate family category can only decrease, if overall immigration decreases. (all numbers are from the Department of Homeland Security Immigration Statistics).

In summary, do we need an immigration policy based on family-sponsored preference? Is such a policy in the interest of the United States or in the interest of the immigrants only?

Is it benefiting the United States? There is ample evidence to the contrary.

Here are some suggested changes to our immigration policy:

1. Phase out family-sponsored immigration except for immediate family (spouse, minor children, parents).
2. End birthright citizenship through a constitutional amendment.
3. Do not consider offering amnesty to some illegal aliens before changes 1 and 2 are enacted.
4. Discontinue diversity immigration.

While the United States faces other large problems in addition to an out-of-hand immigration policy, unless we change our immigration policy it will accelerate and make irreversible the decline of the United States.

In summary, curbing population growth of the United States and the world is the most important issue of the twenty-first century and the key to mitigating climate change, preserving nature's capital, and reducing world poverty.

Afterword

Please keep thinking about these issues. Learn more about them, write to your representatives and other people responsible for policy change, legislation, budgets, and so on. Become active in order to better the future of those who come after us in the United States and everywhere else in the world.

Further Reading (References)

1. Al Gore. *Earth in the Balance.* New York: Rodale, 1992.

   Al Gore. *An Inconvenient Truth.* New York: Rodale, 2006.

2. Jeffrey D. Sachs. *Common Wealth.* New York: Penguin Press, 2008.

3. Robert Engelman. *More: Population, Nature and What Women Want.* Washington, DC: Island Press, 2008.

4. George J. Borjas. *Heaven's Door: Immigration Policy and the American Economy.* Princeton: Princeton University Press, 1999.

5. David Weissbrodt and Laura Danielson. *Immigration Law and Procedure.* 5th ed. Eagan, MN: Thomson&West, 2004.

6. http://www.google.com.